P9-EIF-086

St. Patrick's Day

by Mari C. Schuh

Consulting Editor: Gail Saunders-Smith, Ph.D.

Consultant: Alexa Sandmann, Ed.D.
Professor of Literacy
The University of Toledo
Member, National Council for the Social Studies

Pebble Books

an imprint of Capstone Press
Mankato, Minnesota

Pebble Books are published by Capstone Press
151 Good Counsel Drive, P.O. Box 669, Mankato, Minnesota 56002
http://www.capstone-press.com

1 2 3 4 5 6 07 06 05 04 03 02

Library of Congress Cataloging-in-Publication Data
Schuh, Mari C., 1975–
St. Patrick's Day / by Mari C. Schuh.
p. cm.—(Holidays and celebrations)
Summary: Simple text and photographs describe the history of St. Patrick's Day and the many ways in which it is celebrated.
Includes bibliographical references and index.
ISBN 0-7368-1448-5 (hardcover)
ISBN 0-7368-9404-7 (paperback)
1. Saint Patrick's Day—Juvenile literature. [1. Saint Patrick's Day. 2. Holidays.]
I. Title. II. Series.
GT4995.P3 S37 2003
394.262—dc21 2001008488

Note to Parents and Teachers

The Holidays and Celebrations series supports national social studies standards for units related to culture. This book describes St. Patrick's Day and illustrates how it is celebrated in North America. The images support early readers in understanding the text. The repetition of words and phrases helps early readers learn new words. This book also introduces early readers to subject-specific vocabulary words, which are defined in the Words to Know section. Early readers may need assistance to read some words and to use the Table of Contents, Words to Know, Read More, Internet Sites, and Index/Word List sections of the book.

Table of Contents

March
S M T W T F S
1
2 3 4 5 6 7 8
9 10 11 12 13 14 15
16 17 18 19 20 21 22
23 24 25 26 27 28 29
30 31
South Bay
ST. PATRICK'S DAY PARADE
Hermosa Beach

People celebrate
Saint Patrick's Day
on March 17.

6

Saint Patrick lived
in Ireland hundreds
of years ago. He was
a preacher. He helped
people in Ireland build
churches and schools.

Saint Patrick told stories
about shamrocks.
Today, people decorate
with shamrocks
on Saint Patrick's Day.

Ireland

People wear green clothes
on Saint Patrick's Day.
They remember the
green hills of Ireland.

Some people have parties to celebrate Saint Patrick's Day. They sing and dance. They listen to Irish music.

Some people watch parades on Saint Patrick's Day. Others send cards. Some people make green cakes and cookies.

Students make Saint Patrick's Day crafts in school. They learn about Ireland.

green

leprechaun

pot of gold

shamrocks

The color green, leprechauns, pots of gold, and shamrocks are Saint Patrick's Day symbols.

Happy St. Patrick's Day

People remember Ireland on Saint Patrick's Day. They celebrate with their family and friends.

Words to Know

celebrate—to do something fun on a special occasion

decorate—to add items to a room or an object to make it look nice; people use green items such as shamrocks to decorate for Saint Patrick's Day.

Ireland—a small country in Europe; Ireland is near the countries of Scotland and England.

leprechaun—a make-believe elf that is popular in Irish stories; it was believed that leprechauns would hand over their pot of gold if they were caught.

preacher—a person who teaches religious lessons as a job

shamrock—a clover with three leaves; some shamrocks have four leaves; the shamrock is Ireland's national flower.

Read More

Berendes, Mary. *St. Patrick's Day Shamrocks.* Holiday Symbols. Chanhassen, Minn.: Child's World, 2000.

Margaret, Amy. *St. Patrick's Day.* Library of Holidays. New York: PowerKids Press, 2002.

Vidrine, Beverly Barras. *St. Patrick's Day Alphabet.* Gretna, La.: Pelican Publishing, 2001.

Internet Sites

St. Patrick's Day Crafts for Kids
http://www.enchantedlearning.com/crafts/stpatrick/index.shtml

St. Patrick's Fun at Kids Domain
http://www.kidsdomain.com/holiday/patrick

St. Patrick's Day Resources
http://www.kiddyhouse.com/holidays/stpat

Index/Word List

Word Count: 136
Early-Intervention Level: 14

Credits
Heather Kindseth, series designer; Patrick D. Dentinger, book designer; Wanda Winch, photo researcher; Nancy White, photo stylist

Capstone Press/Gary Sundermeyer, cover, 1, 8, 10, 16, 18 (all), 20
Irish Cultural Centre/Glenn Daly, 12
North Wind Picture Archives, 6
Virginia Scaccionoce, 4
Westrich Photography, 14

Pebble Books thanks Jane Schuette of Belle Plaine, Minnesota, for providing props for photos in this book.